ROCKFORD PUBLIC LIBRARY

Rockford, Illinois

www.rockfordpubliclibrary.org

815-965-9511

Meerkats

by Conrad J. Storad

Lerner Publications Company • Minneapolis

For Natalie. Let books show you the world.

The images in this book are used with the permission of: © age fotostock/SuperStock, pp. 4, 11, 12, 16, 27, 29, 35, 43; © Laura Westlund/Independent Picture Service, p. 5; © Nigel J. Dennis/Photo Researchers, Inc., p. 6; © Wendy Dennis/Visuals Unlimited, pp. 7, 13, 14, 15, 19, 21, 22, 26, 38, 47, 48; © Martin Harvey/Peter Arnold, Inc., pp. 8, 9, 37; © Henry Horenstein/CORBIS, p. 10; © Getty Images, pp. 17, 30, 34, 46; © Gunter Ziesler/Peter Arnold, Inc., p. 18; © Clem Haagner, Gallo Images/CORBIS, p. 20; © Paul A. Souders/CORBIS, p. 23; © Peter Johnson/CORBIS, p. 24; © D. MacDonald/OSF/Animals Animals, pp. 25, 31; © Martin Harvey/CORBIS, p. 28; © Clem Haagner/Photo Researchers, Inc., pp. 32, 33; © Dr. John D. Cunningham/Visuals Unlimited, p. 36; © Joe McDonald/Visuals Unlimited, p. 39; © Steve & Ann Toon/Robert Harding World Imagery/Corbis, p. 40; © Ken Lucas/Visuals Unlimited, p. 41; © Rainer Jensen/dpa/Corbis, p. 42.

Front Cover: © age fotostock/SuperStock

Website address: www.lernerbooks.com

Lerner Publications Company
A division of Lerner Publishing Group
241 First Avenue North
Minneapolis, Minnesota 55401 U.S.A.

Library of Congress Cataloging-in-Publication Data

Storad, Conrad J.
    Meerkats / by Conrad J. Storad.
        p.   cm. — (Early bird nature books)
    Includes index.
    ISBN-13: 978–0–8225–6466–9 (lib. bdg. : alk. paper)
    ISBN-10: 0–8225–6466–1 (lib. bdg. : alk. paper)
    1. Meerkat—Juvenile literature. I. Title.
QL737.C235S76 2007
599.74'2—dc22   2006030161

Manufactured in the United States of America
1 2 3 4 5 6 – JR – 12 11 10 09 08 07

Contents

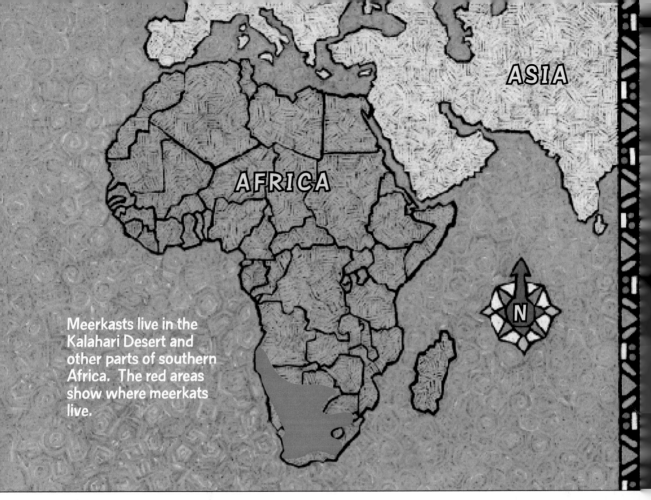

ASIA

AFRICA

Meerkasts live in the Kalahari Desert and other parts of southern Africa. The red areas show where meerkats live.

N

Be a Word Detective

Can you find these words as you read about the meerkat's life? Be a detective and try to figure out what they mean. You can turn to the glossary on page 46 for help.

dens	**mob**	**prey**
desert	**nictitating**	**sentries**
gang	**membrane**	**territory**
kits	**nursing**	**venom**

Chapter 1

The meerkat's scientific name is Suricata suricatta. Meerkats are also called suricates. What is a group of meerkats called?

What Is a Meerkat?

The meerkats are busy. Some are standing tall, watching for danger. Some are digging in the ground. Others are taking care of baby meerkats. The rest are looking for food. Another long, hot day has begun.

Meerkats are members of a group of animals called mongooses. Mongooses have long bodies, four short legs, and long tails. Many kinds of mongooses live alone. Others live in small groups. Meerkats live together in large groups. A group of meerkats is called a gang. A meerkat gang has up to 30 members.

Meerkats are small animals. A full-grown adult meerkat weighs 2 to 3 pounds. When it stands up straight on its hind legs, it is only about 12 inches tall. That is as tall as a ruler standing on its end.

When a meerkat stands on all four feet, it is only about 6 inches high. It is about half as tall as a house cat.

Meerkats often stand up on their back legs. When a meerkat stands on two legs, its stiff tail helps it balance.

A meerkat has a pointed snout with lots of tiny, sharp teeth. It has small ears and eyes. Around each eye is a patch of dark hair.

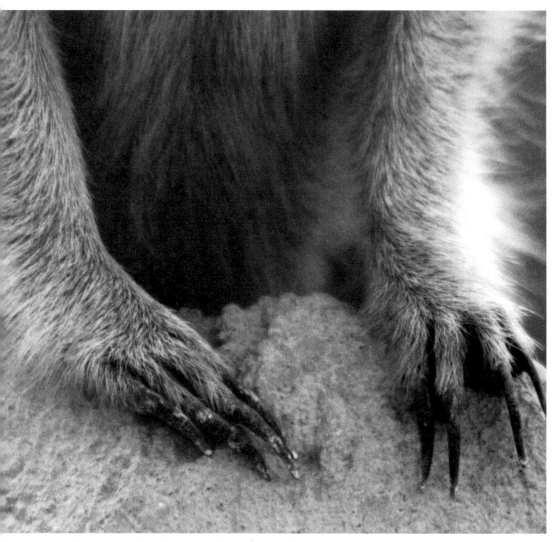

A meerkat's claws are long and sharp.

Meerkats have four toes on each foot. The toes on the front feet have long claws. Meerkats use their claws for digging and climbing.

A meerkat's hair can be gray, tan, brown, or rusty orange. It can have gray or tan stripes. The tip of a meerkat's tail is dark-colored. No two meerkats look exactly the same.

Meerkats have dark stripes on their backs.

Chapter 2

These meerkats are peeking out of a hole in the ground. Where do meerkats live?

Desert Dwellers

Meerkats live in southern Africa. Some live in the Kalahari Desert. Others live in dry grasslands. The area where meerkats live spreads over 1 million square miles. That is almost four times as big as the state of Texas!

Some meerkats live in grasslands that have only a few trees.

Parts of the Kalahari Desert are very dry.

In the Kalahari Desert, the sun shines hot and bright. Shade is hard to find. It does not rain very often.

The desert has patches of tough grass. It has some small trees and thorny bushes. But most of the desert is covered with sandy or rocky ground. The ground is white, tan, gray, or brownish orange.

A meerkat's hair matches the color of the sandy ground. This coloring helps meerkats hide from predators (PREH-duh-turz). Predators are animals that hunt and eat other animals.

These meerkats are the same color as the ground. From far away, it would be hard to see them.

Meerkats see very well. They can spot predators that are far away.

The dark patches around a meerkat's eyes act like built-in sunglasses. The patches help meerkats see in the bright sun. Meerkats' eyes also have a nictitating membrane (NIHK-tuh-tay-tihng MEHM-brayn). The nictitating membrane is like a thin skin between the eye and the eyelid. The nictitating membrane works like a windshield wiper. It sweeps away sand and dirt each time the meerkat blinks.

Summer days in the Kalahari Desert are hot. The nights are chilly. So meerkats dig dens under the ground to live in. Each den has several rooms. The rooms stay cool in the daytime and warm at night. Tunnels connect the rooms. Other tunnels lead to entrances.

Three baby meerkats are coming out of their den.

The den is a safe place. If a predator comes near,
the meerkats can hide inside the den.

A den may have many entrances. A mound
of dirt or sand surrounds each entrance hole.
This dirt piled up when the meerkats dug the den.

Groups of meerkats sleep together in the
den. In summer, the animals spread out to stay
cool. In winter, they cuddle together in piles.
They keep one another warm.

Meerkats don't have much hair on their bellies. Sunlight can shine through the hair. It warms up the meerkats' skin.

On cold mornings, meerkats crawl out of their warm dens. They stand facing the sun. They look like students waiting for a school bus. But they are really warming up to start the day. A meerkat's belly has a patch of dark skin. The dark skin soaks up the sun's heat. It warms the meerkat's body.

Chapter 3

Each group of meerkats has its own neighborhood. What is a gang's neighborhood called?

Anytime Is Chow Time

 Each gang of meerkats lives in its own territory (TAYR-uh-tor-ee). The territory is the gang's neighborhood. Territories are large areas of land. A gang's territory may cover 2 or 3 square miles. That is bigger than 1,000 football fields side by side!

Each gang keeps other gangs out of its territory.

A meerkat usually eats food when it finds it. But the meerkat may save some food for other members of the gang. This meerkat has caught a lizard.

Meerkats need a big territory so they can find plenty of food to eat. Meerkats are always hungry. They eat every few minutes as long as they can find food.

A gang has up to five different dens in its territory. The meerkats stay in one den for a while. They stay until they run out of food and water. Then the gang moves to another den.

Baby meerkats can't walk far. When the gang moves from one den to another, adults carry the babies.

Meerkats eat the roots and fruit of some kinds of plants. But mostly they eat small animals such as insects, lizards, and birds. The animals that a meerkat hunts are called its prey.

These meerkats are hunting for small animals to eat.

This young meerkat is pouncing on a scorpion.

A hungry meerkat can eat dozens of big beetles and hundreds of ants in one day. Meerkats eat termites, worms, lizards, bird eggs, and spiders. They also hunt for centipedes, crickets, grasshoppers, mice, and small snakes.

When a meerkat catches a scorpio̸͟t̸es off the scorpion's stinger. Then the meerkat can e̸͟t̸͟t̸ being stung.

Meerkats even hunt scorpions. Scorpions are relatives of spiders. A scorpion's tail has a sharp stinger. The stinger is full of venom. Venom is a kind of poison. A scorpion's venom can kill some small animals. But meerkats are not afraid of scorpions. A scorpion's venom will not hurt a meerkat. Meerkats munch on scorpions as if they were crunchy potato chips.

Meerkats hunt near their den. They walk along, sniffing the ground. Sometimes they chase small animals that are hiding on the ground. But most of a meerkat's favorite kinds of food live underground.

Meerkats can smell food that is under the ground.

When meerkats smell food under the ground, they use their sharp claws to dig for it. The claws work like shovels. Meerkats dig very fast. They can move pounds of dirt in just a few seconds. Sand and dirt flies in every direction until the meerkat finds its prey.

Meerkats can close their ears when they dig. That way, sand and dirt don't get in their ears.

In very dry areas, meerkats may go a long time without drinking water.

Like all animals, meerkats need water to survive. But the places where meerkats live are very dry. Water is hard to find. Sometimes meerkats can drink water from puddles or streams. But meerkats get most of the water they need from their food.

Chapter 4

Meerkats take good care of their babies. What are baby meerkats called?

Growing Up

 Female meerkats usually have two to four babies at one time. Baby meerkats are called kits. The kits have almost no hair when they are born. Their eyes are closed.

Newborn kits stay in the den. There the babies are safe from predators. The kits drink their mother's milk. This is called nursing. They grow strong.

Two kits are drinking their mother's milk.

Adult meerkats take turns being babysitters.

When they are about three weeks old, the kits go outside for the first time. But they don't go far from the den. Older meerkats work as babysitters. They stay with the kits and keep them safe. Sometimes the babysitters give the babies tasty beetles or worms to eat. As the kits get older, they try to catch their own bug snacks.

As the kits grow up, they start to hunt for their own food. This kit has found a big beetle.

Kits love to play with their brothers and sisters.

When the kits are about four months old, each one gets its own teacher. The teachers show the kits how to hunt for food. They teach them how to watch for danger. They teach the kits everything they need to know about being meerkats. When the kits are six months old, they are grown up. They are ready to go to work for the gang.

Meerkats live to be up to 10 years old.

Chapter 5

Meerkats are always watching for danger. What do meerkats do when they want to see a long way?

Beware the Mob

 The desert is a dangerous place to live. But all of the meerkats in a gang work together. They help one another to survive.

Some meerkats work as sentries (SEHN-treez). Sentries guard the area around the den. They watch out for danger while other meerkats hunt for food.

This sentry has climbed a tree.

Sentries may stand on a pile of dirt. Sometimes they climb into the branches of a small tree. Sometimes they stand on top of tall rocks. When they are up high, meerkats can see a long way.

Jackals are relatives of dogs and wolves.

The sentries watch for predators such as foxes, jackals, and hyenas (hy-EE-nuhz). They also watch the sky for hawks and eagles. All of these animals hunt meerkats. When a sentry sees danger, it barks to warn the rest of the gang. The sentry barks louder and louder as the enemy gets closer.

The members of the gang run to the den to hide from the predator. The sentries may dig up the ground to make clouds of dust. The dust helps the meerkats hide from the predator.

This bird is a martial (MAR-shuhl) eagle. It has killed a goose. Martial eagles hunt meerkats too.

Meerkats crowd together when they see a predator.

If the predator doesn't leave, the meerkats work together to drive it away. The meerkats crowd close together. The tightly packed bunch of meerkats is called a mob.

Each member of the mob faces the predator. The meerkats stand up tall and hold their tails straight and stiff. They puff up their hair. Each little meerkat tries to look as large as possible. The meerkats are close together, so the mob looks like one big animal.

The mob charges at the predator. The meerkats leap into the air at the same time. They growl and hiss.

A meerkat looks much bigger when it puffs up its hair.

The predator may get scared and run away. But it may keep attacking. Then the meerkats bite and scratch the predator. One little meerkat can't fight off a predator. But working together, the mob is strong enough to drive the animal away.

Meerkats have sharp teeth. They bite predators to make them go away.

The meerkats in a gang work together. They keep one another safe.

The Kalahari Desert is home for meerkats. But the desert is also a dangerous place to live. To stay alive, meerkats have to stick together and stand tall.

A NOTE TO ADULTS
ON SHARING A BOOK

When you share a book with a child, you show that reading is important. To get the most out of the experience, read in a comfortable, quiet place. Turn off the television and limit other distractions, such as telephone calls.

Be prepared to start slowly. Take turns reading parts of this book. Stop occasionally and discuss what you're reading. Talk about the photographs. If the child begins to lose interest, stop reading. When you pick up the book again, revisit the parts you have already read.

BE A VOCABULARY DETECTIVE

The word list on page 5 contains words that are important in understanding the topic of this book. Be word detectives and search for the words as you read the book together. Talk about what the words mean and how they are used in the sentence. Do any of these words have more than one meaning? You will find the words defined in a glossary on page 46.

WHAT ABOUT QUESTIONS?

Use questions to make sure the child understands the information in this book. Here are some suggestions:

> What did this paragraph tell us? What does this picture show? What is a group of meerkats called? Where do meerkats live? How do meerkats stay warm on cold nights? How do baby meerkats learn how to hunt for food? How do meerkats make predators go away? What is your favorite part of the book? Why?

If the child has questions, don't hesitate to respond with questions of your own, such as What do *you* think? Why? What is it that you don't know? If the child can't remember certain facts, turn to the index.

INTRODUCING THE INDEX

The index helps readers find information without searching through the whole book. Turn to the index on page 48. Choose an entry such as *eating* and ask the child to use the index to find out what meerkats eat. Repeat with as many entries as you like. Ask the child to point out the differences between an index and a glossary. (The index helps readers find information, while the glossary tells readers what words mean.)

MEERKATS

BOOKS

Halfmann, Janet. *Mongoose*. Detroit: Kidhaven Press, 2005. This book has lots of information about mongooses, animals that are relatives of meerkats.

Johnson, Rebecca L. *A Walk in the Desert*. Minneapolis: Lerner Publications, 2001. Learn about life in a North American desert.

Landau, Elaine. *Desert Mammals*. New York: Children's Press, 1996. Find out how different animals have adapted to living in deserts.

MacQuitty, Miranda. *Desert*. New York: Dorling Kindersley, 2000. This book has interesting information about deserts around the world.

Moore, Heidi. *A Mob of Meerkats*. Chicago: Heinemann Library, 2004. Find out more about life in a mob of meerkats.

WEBSITES

Mammals: Meerkats in the Wild
http://homepage.mac.com/rstacy/meerkatswild.html
This website has a wide variety of photos of meerkats playing, hunting, and more.

The Meerkat Mpango
http://www.meerkat.org/
This website has lots of information about meerkats, along with photos and links.

Meerkats
http://whozoo.org/students/kartho/meerkat3.htm
This Web page has information about the meerkats living at the Fort Worth, Texas, zoo.

Sights and Sounds from Stand Tall: Meerkats
http://magma.nationalgeographic.com/ngm/0209/sights_n_sounds/media1.html
This National Geographic page has a short Flash movie of meerkats, complete with meerkat sounds.

GLOSSARY

dens: meerkats' underground homes. Each den is made up of several rooms and tunnels.

desert: a place that gets very little rain

gang: a group of meerkats that live together

kits: baby meerkats

mob: a group of meerkats standing close together to fight an enemy

nictitating membrane (NIHK-tuh-tay-tihng MEHM-brayn): a thin skin underneath a meerkat's eyelid. It works like a windshield wiper to clean dirt out of the meerkat's eye.

nursing: drinking mother's milk

prey: the animals a meerkat hunts for food

sentries (SEHN-treez): meerkats that guard the den. They watch out for animals that hunt and eat meerkats.

territory (TAYR-uh-tor-ee): the area of land where a group of meerkats lives and hunts for food

venom: a kind of poison

INDEX

Pages listed in **bold** type refer to photographs.